OPERA JOURNEYS

Giuseppe Verdi's

AIDA

COMPLETE LIBRETTO
with Music Highlight examples

Edited by Burton D. Fisher
Principal lecturer, *Opera Journeys Lecture Series*

Opera Journeys Publishing™/ Boca Raton, Florida

WEBSITE: www.operajourneys.com
EMAIL: operaj@bellsouth.net

Aida

Opera in Italian in four acts

Music

by

Giuseppe Verdi

Libretto by Antonio Ghislanzoni

Premiere in Cairo on Christmas Eve

December 24, 1871

Libretto

AIDA

ACT I - Scene 1

Prelude: Aida's theme

Andante mosso

Prelude: Priest's theme

Andante mosso

A Grand Hall in the Palace of Pharaoh in the ancient Egyptian city of Memphis.
The scene is dominated by large colonnades and statues of the gods;
in the background, the temples and palaces of Memphis and the pyramids.

(Radames converses with Ramphis, the High Priest)

Ramfis:
Si: corre voce che l'Etiope ardisca sfidarci ancora, e del Nilo la valle e tebe minacciar. Fra breve un messo recherà il ver.

Ramphis:
Yes, there is a report that the Ethiopians dare defy us, and threaten the Nile valley and Thebes. Soon a messenger will bring news.

Radames:
La sacra Iside consultasti?

Radames:
Did you consult the sacred Isis?

Ramfis:
Ella ha nomato dell'Egizie falangi il condottier supremo.

Ramphis:
She has named the supreme leader of the Egyptian troops.

Radames:
Oh lui felice!

Radames:
Oh! What a fortunate man!

Ramfis:
Giovane e prode è desso. Ora del Nume reco i decreti al Re.

Ramphis:
He is young and brave. Now I go to the Pharaoh to convey the decrees of the goddess.

(Ramphis exits)

Radames:
Se quel guerrier io fossi!
Se il mio sogno s'avverasse!
Un esercito di prodi da me guidato

Radames:
If I could be chosen that warrior,
my dream would be fulfilled:
a proud army led to victory by me,

e la vittoria... e il plauso di Menfi tutta!	and the applause of all Memphis.
E a te, mia dolce Aida, tornar di lauri cinto,	And to return to you, my gentle Aida,
dirti: per te ho pugnato,	crowned with laurels, to tell you that I have
per te ho vinto!	fought and been victorious for you!

Andantino

Ce - le - ste Ai - da,   for - ma di - vi - na,

Celeste Aida, forma divina.	Heavenly Aida, divinely beautiful.
Mistico serto di luce e fior,	Mystical vision of flower and sunlight,
del mio pensiero tu sei regina,	you reign over my thoughts;
tu di mia vita sei lo splendor.	you are the splendor of my life.
Il tuo bel cielo vorrei ridarti,	I would restore you to your bright skies,
le dolci brezze del patria suol;	and the soft breezes of your native soil;
un regal serta sul crin posarti,	I would place a regal crown on you,
ergerti un trono vicino al sol, ah!	raise a throne for you near the sun, ah!
Celeste Aida, forma divina,	Heavenly Aida, divinely beautiful.
Mistico raggio di luce e fior.....	Mystical vision of flower and sunlight...

(Amneris enters)

Allegro assai moderato

Amneris:
Quale insolita gioia nel tuo sguardo!
Di quale nobil fierezza ti balena il volto!
Degna d'invidia, quanto saria la donna il
cui bramato aspetto tanta luce di gaudio in te
destasse!

Amneris:
What unusual joy in your glance!
What noble pride glows in your face!
Would I be the woman for whose love you
are yearning, and has awakened you to
light and happiness!

Radames:
D'un sogno avventuroso si beava il mio
cuore.
Oggi, la Diva proferse il nome del guerrier
che al campo le schiere egizie condurrà.
Ah! s'io fossi a tal onor prescelto.

Radames:
I had an adventurous dream that was
stirring my heart.
Today, the goddess will declare the name of
the warrior who shall lead the Egyptians.
Ah! If I was selected for such an honor.

Amneris:
Nè un altro sogno mai più gentil, più soave,
al core ti parlo?
Non hai tu in Menfi desideri...speranze?

Amneris:
Is there another dream, more gentle, more
sweet, speaking in your heart?
Have you dreams and hopes in Memphis?

Radames:
Io! (Quale inchiesta!)
(Forse l'arcano amore scopri che m'arde in
core della tua schiava il nome mi lesse nel
pensier!)

Radames:
I! (What a question!)
(Perhaps she has discovered the secret love
in my heart, and reads that her slave's
name is in my thoughts!)

Amneris:
(Oh guai! Se un altro amore ardesse a lui
nel core!)

Amneris:
(Oh! Woe if another love burns in his
heart!)

Radames:
(Della sua schiava il nome mi lesse nel
pensier!)

Radames:
(Does she read her slave's name in my
thoughts?)

Amneris:
(Guai se il mio sguardo penetra questo fatal
mister!)

Amneris:
(Woe, if my could penetrate this fatal
mystery!)

Radames:
(Forse mi lesse nel pensier!)

Radames:
(Perhaps she reads my thoughts!)

(Aida enters)
Radames:
Dessa!

Radames:
It is her!

Amneris:
(Ei si turba... e quale sguardo rivolse a lei!
Aida!... a me rivale forse saria costei?)

Vieni, o diletta, appresati,
schiava non sei nè ancella, qui, dove in
dolce fascino io ti chiamai sorella.
Piangi? Delle tue lacrime svela il segreto a
me.

Amneris:
(He is moved...and what a look he gives
her! Aida! Is she my rival for him?)
(turning to Aida)
Come, dearest friend, come near to me,
I no longer call you slave; here with gentle
affection I call you my sister.
You weep? Tell me the secret behind your
tears.

Aida:
Ohimè! di guerra fremere l'atroce grido io
sento. Per l'infelice patria, per me per voi pavento.

Aida:
Alas! I hear the atrocious shouts of vicious
battle. I tremble for my unhappy homeland.

Amneris:
Favelli il ver?

Amneris:
Do you speak the truth?

N'e s'agita più grave cura in te?
(Trema, o rea schiava!)

There is nothing more grave in your heart?
(Tremble, damned slave!)

Radames:
(Nel volto a lei balena.)

Radames: *(looking at Aida)*
(There is a spark in her.)

Allegro agitato e presto

Amneris:
(Ah! Trema, rea schiave, trema!)

Amneris:
Ah! Tremble, damned slave, tremble!)

Radames:
(Lo sdegno ed il sospetto)

Radames:
(There is disdain and suspicion.)

Amneris:
(Ch'io nel tuo cor discenda!)

Amneris:
(That I might arouse your heart!)

Radames:
(Guai se l'arcano affetto a noi leggesse in core!)

Radames:
(Woe if she reads the secret love we have in our hearts!)

Amneris:
(Trema che il ver m'apprenda quel pianto e quel rossor!)

Amneris:
(Tremble that I may know the truth of your tears and your blushing!

Radames:
(Guai se leggesse in cor!)

Radames:
(Woe if she reads our hearts!)

Aida:
(Ah! no, sulla mia patria
non geme il cor soltanto;
quello ch'io verso è pianto di sventurato amor!)

Aida:
(Ah! No, in my heart I grieve not for my country;
those tears that pour from me are tears of unfortunte love!)

Radames:
(Nel volto a lei balena lo sdegno ed il sospetto.
Guai se l'arcano affetto a noi leggesse in cor!)

Radames:
(In her look she has disdain and dark suspicion.
Woe if she reads the secret love that is in our hearts!)

Amneris:
(Rea schiava, trema!
Ch'io nel tuo cor discenda!
Ah! trema che il ver m'apprenda
quel pianto e quel rossor!)

Amneris:
(Damned slave, tremble!
Could I be the one your heart despises!
Ah! Tremble that I may know the truth of
your tears and your blushing!)

The Pharaoh enters, preceded by his guards, and followed by Ramphis, Ministers,
Priests, Captains and Officers..

Il Re:
Alta cagion v'aduna, o fidi Egizi,
al vostro Re d'intorno.
Dai confin d'Etiopia un Messaggero
dianzi giungea.
Gravi novelle ei reca.
Vi piaccia udirlo.
Il Messagger s'avanzi!

Pharaoh:
A great cause summons you around your
Pharaoh, faithful Egyptians.
A Messenger has arrived from the interior
of Ethiopia.
He brings grave news.
Please hear him.
Let the Messenger come forward!

Messaggero:
Il sacro suolo dell'Egitto è invaso
dai barbari Etiopi.
I nostri campi fu devastati...
arse le messi... e baldi della facil vittoria,
i predatori già marciano su Tebe!

Messenger:.
The sacred soil of Egypt has been invaded
by the barbarous Ethiopians.
Our fields are devastated...
the crops burned...and emboldened by their
easy victory, the predators march on Thebes.

Radames, Il Re, Ramfis, Sacerdoti,
Ministri, Capitani:
Ed osan tanto!

Radames, Pharaoh, Ramphis, Priests,
Ministers, Captains:
They dare such!

Messaggero:
Un guerriero indomabile, feroce,
li conduce, Amonasro.

Messenger;
An indomitable and ferocious warrior leads
them: Amonasro.

Radames, Il Re, Ramfis, Sacerdoti,
Ministri, Capitani:
Il Re!

Radames, Pharaoh, Ramphis, Priests,
Ministers, Captains:
The King!

Aida:
(Mio padre!)

Aida:
(My father!)

Messaggero:
Già Tebe è in armi e dalle cento porte
sul barbaro invasore proromperà, guerra
recando e morte.

Messenger:
Thebes is already armed, attacked by the
barbarians from a hundred gates, all
shouting war and death.

Il Re:
Sì: guerra e morte il nostro grido sia!

Pharaoh:
Let war and death be our cry!

Ramfis:
Guerra!

Ramphis:
War!

**Radames, Il Re, Ramfis, Sacerdoti,
Ministri, Capitani:**
Guerra! Guerra! Tremenda! inesorata!

**Radames, Pharaoh, Ramphis, Priests,
Ministers, Captains:**
War! War! Tremendous! Inexorable!

Il Re:
Iside venerata di nostre schiere invite
già designava il condottier supremo:
Radames!

Pharaoh: *(Addressing Radames)*
Venerated Isis has already designated the
supreme leader of our armies:
Radames!

Aida. Amneris, Ministri, Capitani:
Radames!

Aida, Amneris, Ministers, Captains:
Radames!

Radames:
Ah! Sien grazie a Numi!
Son paghi i voti miei!

Radames:
Ah! Thanks to the gods!
I have been rewarded for my prayers!

Amneris:
(Ei duce!)

Amneris:
He leads us!

Aida:
(Io tremo!)

Aida:
(I tremble!)

Ministri, Capitani:
Radames! Radames! Radames! Radames!

Ministers, Captains:
Radames! Radames! Radames! Radames!

Il Re:
Or di Vulcano al tempio muovi, o guerrier;
le sacre armi ti cingi e alla vittoria vola.

Pharaoh:
Now warrior, go to the temple of Vulcan,
and receive the sacred arms and blessings
of victory.

Su! del Nilo al sacro lido
accorrete, Egizi eroi,
da'ogni cor prorompa il grido:
guerra e morte, morte allo stranier!

Arise! From the sacred shores of the Nile,
hurry, heroic Egyptians,
from every heart give the cry:
war and death to the foreigner!

Ramfis:
Gloria ai Numi! Ognun rammenti
ch'essi reggono gli eventi,
che in poter de'Numi solo stan le sorti del
guerrier.

Ramphis:
Glory to the gods. All remember that
they rule events,
that in the power of the gods rests the fate
of the warrior.

Ministri, Capitani:
Su! del Nilo al sacro lido
sian barriera i nostri petti;
non echeggi che un sol grido:
guerra, guerra e morte allo stranier!

Ministers, Captains:
Arise! From the sacred shores of the Nile,
our breasts will be a barrier.
Let there be but one cry:
war, war, and death to the foreigner!

Il Re:
Su! su! del Nilo al sacro lido
accorrete, Egizi eroi;
da ogni cor prorompa un grido:
Guerra e morte allo stranier!

Pharaoh:
Arise! from the sacred shores of the Nile,
hurry, heroic Egyptians,
from every heart give the cry:
war and death to the foreigner!

Aida:
(Per chi piango? Per chi prego?
Qual poter m'avvince a lui!
Deggio amarlo ed è costui un nemico, uno
stranier!)

Aida:
(For whom do I weep! For whom do I pray!
What is the power that binds me to him!
I must love him and yet he is an enemy, an
alien!)

Radames:
Sacro fremito di gloria tutta l'anima
m'investe.
Su! corriamo alla vittoria!
Guerra e morte allo stranier!

Radames:
Sacred stirrings of glory have invested my
soul.
Arise! Let's rush to victory!
War and death to the foreigner!

Amneris:
Di mia man ricevi, o duce,
il vessillo glorioso;
ti sia guida, ti sia luce
della gloria sul sentier.

Amneris: *(to Radames)*
Receive from me, o leader,
the glorious standard;
it will guide you, and be a light on your
path to glory.

Il Re:
Su! del Nilo al sacro lido.........

Pharaoh:
Arise! From the sacred shores of the Nile..

Ramfis, Sacerdoti:
Gloria ai Numi! Ognun rammenti....

Ramphis, Priests:
Glory to the gods! All remember.....

Ministri, Capitani:
Su! del Nilo al sacro lido........

Ministers, Captains:
Arise! From the sacred shores of the Nile..

Radames e Messaggero:
Su! corriamo, su!

Radames, Messenger:
Arise! We rush to victory!

Amneris:
Ti sia guida, ti sia luce della gloria sul
sentier.

Amneris:
That this may guide you and light your path
to glory.

Aida:
(Per chi piango? Per chi prego?)

Aida:
(For whom do I weep! For whom do I pray?)

Il Re e Ramfis:
Guerra!

Pharaoh and Ramphis:
War!

Sacerdoti, Ministri, Capitani:
Guerra! Guerra! Guerra!

Priests, Ministers, Captains:
War! War! War!

Aida:
(Deggia amarlo, e veggo in lui un nemico,
uno stranier!)

Aida:
(I must love him, and he is an enemy, an
alien!)

Tutti Gli Altri:
Guerra! Guerra! Stermino all'invasor!

All:
War! War! Exterminate the invader!

Amneris:
Ritorna vincitor!

Amneris: *(to Radames)*
Return victorious!

Ri - tor - na vin - ci - tor!   Ri - tor - na vin - ci - tor!

Tutti:
Ritorna vincitor!

All:
Return victorious!

(All leave. Aida is alone)

Aida:
Ritorna vincitor!
E dal mio labbro uscì l'empia parola!
Vincitor del padre mio...
di lui che impugna l'armi per me...
per ridonarmi una patria, una reggia,
e il nome il lustre che qui celar m'è forza!

Aida:
Return victorious!
And from my lips those impious words!
Victory for my father......
who has waged war for me....
to return me to my country, my realm,
and my lineage that I am forced to conceal.

Vincitor de' miei fratelli... ond'io lo vegga,
tinto del sangue amato, trionfar nel plauso
dell'Egizie coorti!
E dietro il carro, un Re... mio padre... di
catene avvinto!

Victory for my brothers...who I see soiled
in loving blood, defeated by the Egyptian
armies!
And behind the chariot, the king, my father,
bound in chains!

L'insana parola, o Numi, sperdete!
al seno d'un padre la figlia rendete;
struggete le squadre, dei nostri oppressor!

The insane words, o gods, forget them!
At a sign from my father, his daughter
returns, the squadrons of our oppressors
destroyed!

Ah! sventurata! Che dissi?
E l'amor mio?
Dunque scordar poss'io questo fervido
amore che, oppressa e schiava, come raggio
di sol qui mi beava?

Ah! Unhappy one! What did I say?
And my love?
How can I forget that fervid love that
oppresses and enslaves me, like a ray of
sun that blesses me?

Imprecherò la morte a Radames...
a lui ch'amo pur tanto?
Ah! Non fu in terra mai da più crudeli
angosce un core affranto!

Shall I pray for the death of Radames...
whom I love so much?
Ah! There was never on earth a more cruel
anguish and such a broken heart!

I sacri nomi di padre d'amante,
né proferir poss'io, né ricordar.
Per l'un... per l'altro... confusa, tremante,
io piangere vorrei, vorrei pregar.
Ma la mia prece in bestemmia si muta...
delitto è il pianto a me, colpa il sospir.
In notte cupa la mente è perduta...
e nell'ansia crudel vorrei morir.
Numi, pietà del mio soffrir!
Speme non v'ha pel mio dolor.
Amor fatal, tremendo amor
spezzami il cor, fammi morir!
Numi, pietà del mio soffrir!

Sacred gods of my loving father,
I cannot utter, nor remember.
For one..for the other..confused, trembling.
I want to weep, I want to pray.
But my prayers are blasphemy...
my tears a crime, my sighs a wrong.
In the dense night, my mind is lost...
and in this cruel anxiety I want to die.
Gods, mercy on my suffering!
There is no hope in my pain.
Fatal love, powerful love
breaks my heart. I want to die!
Gods! Have mercy on my suffering!

Cantabile

Nu - mi, pie - tà   del   mio   sof - frir!

ACT I - Scene 2

Interior of the sacred Temple of Vulcan at Memphis. There is an altar, statues of deities, emblems, and tripods with incense burning.

Andante con moto

Pos - sen - te, possen - te Fthà,

Sacerdotesse. Sacerdoti, Ramfis:
Possente, possente Fthà, del mondo
Spirito animator, ah!
Noi t'invochiamo!
Tu che dal nulla hai tratto
L'onde, la terra, il ciel.
Noi t'invochiamo!
Immenso, immenso Fthà,
del mondo spirito fecondator, ah!
Noi t'invochiamo!

Nume che del tuo spirito sei figlio e genitor,
Noi t'invochiamo!
Fuoco increato, eterno.
Onde ebbe luce il sol, ah!
Noi t'invochiamo!
Vita dell'universo, mito d'eterno amor,
Noi t'invochiam!
Immenso Fthà!
Noi t'invochiam!

Priestesses, Priests, Ramphis:
All-powerful, all-powerful Phthà,
animating spirit of the world, ah!
We invoke you!
You who have created the waves,
the land, the heavens.
We invoke you!
All-powerful Phthà.
Spirit that created the world. Ah!
We invoke you!

God whose spirit is both son and father,
we invoke you!
Creator of fire, from which the sun has its
light, Ah!
We invoke you!
Life of the universe, gift of eternal love,
we invoke you!
All-powerful Phthà!
We invoke you!

Sacred dance of the Priestesses. Radames enters, unarmed, and approaches the altar where the Priestesses place a silver veil on his head.

Sacerdotesse:
Immenso Fthà!

Priestesses:
All-powerful Phthà!

Ramfis, Sacerdoti:
Noi t'invochiam!

Ramphis, Priests:
We invoke you!

Ramfis:
Mortal, diletto ai Numi, a te fidate
son d'Egitto le sorti.

Ramphis: _(to Radames)_
Mortal, beloved of the gods, to you the fate
of Egypt is committed.

Il sacro brando dal Dio temprato, per tua
man diventi.
Ai nemici terror, folgore, morte.

Sacerdoti:
Il sacro brando dal Dio temprato......

Ramfis:
... folgore, morte,

Nume, custode e vindice,
di questa sacra terra. La mano tua distendi
sovra l'Egizio suol.

Radames:
Nume, che duce ed arbitro sei d'ogni
umana guerra, proteggi tu, difendi d'Egitto
il sacro suol.

Sacerdoti, Ramfis:
Nume, custode e vindice........

Radames:
Proteggi tu, difendi d'Egitto il sacro suol.

Sacerdotesse:
Possente Fthà,
Del mondo creator, ah!
Possente Fthà,
Spirito animator,
Spirito fecondator,
Immenso Fthà!

Radames:
Possente Fthà!

The sacred sword, tempered by god, will
rise in your hand.
Strike the enemy with terror and death.

Priests:
The sacred sword, tempered by god.....

Ramphis:
...strike death.
(turns to the statue of the god)
God, leader and judge,
from this sacred land you have spread your
hand over Egyptian soil.

Radames:
God, who is leader and judge of every
human war, protect and defend sacred
Egyptian soil.

Priests , Ramphis::
God, leader and judge.........

Radames:
Protect and defend sacred Egyptian soil.

*(While Radames is being vested with the
consecrated armor, the Priests and
Priestesses resume the religious hymn and
mystic dance.)*

Priestesses:
All-powerful Phthà!
Creator of the world, ah!
All-powerful Phthà!
Animating spirit,
Progenitor spirit,
All-powerful Phthà!

Radames:
All-powerful Phthà!

ACT II - Scene 1

Amneris's apartments. Amneris is surrounded by female dlaves who adorn her for the triumphal celebration, and Moorish slave boys dance.

Schiave:
Chi mai fra gl'inni e i plausi
erge alla gloria il vol.
Al par d'un Dio terribile,
fulgente al par del sol!
Vieni: sul crin ti piovano
contesti al lauri i fior:
Suonin di gloria i cantici
coi cantici d'amor.

Slave Girls:
Who raises your wishes to glory with
hymns and praise.
Equal to a terrible,
resplendent as the sun!
Come: on your tresses rain
laurels and flowers.
Sing the songs of glory
with the songs of love.

Cantabile

Ah! Vie - ni, vieni, amor mio m'ineb - ria,
Ah! Come, come my love, intoxicate me,

Amneris:
(Ah! Vieni, viene amor mio, m'inebria,
fammi beato il cor!)

Amneris:
(Ah! Come, my love, intoxicate me,
make my heart beat!)

Schiave:
Or dove son le barbare
orde dello stranier?
Siccome nebbia sparvero
al soffio del guerrier.
Vieni: di gloria il premio
Raccogli, o vincitor;
T'arrise la vittoria,
T'arriderà l'amor.

Slave Girls:
Now where are those barbarian
hordes of foreigners?
They scatter like the mist
at the breath of the warrior.
Come o conqueror and gather
the reward of glory.
Victory smiled upon you,
love will smile upon you.

Amneris:
(Ah! Vieni, vieni amor mio, ravvivami
d'un caro accento ancor!)

Amneris:
(Ah! Come, my love, revive me
again with the sweet sound of your voice!)

Schiave::
Vieni; sul crin ti piovano
contesti ai lauri i fior.
Suonin di gloria i cantici
coi cantici d'amor.

Slave Girls:
Come; on your tresses rain
laurels and flowers.
Sing the songs of glory
with the songs of love.

Amneris:
(Ah! Vieni, vieni amor mio, m'inebria,
fammi beato il cor!)

Silenzio! Aida verso noi s'avanza.
Figlia dei vinti, il suo dolor m'è sacro.

Amneris:
(Ah! Come, my love, intoxicate me,
Make my heart beat!)

Silence! Aida approaches us.
Daughter of the vanquished, her grief is
sacred to me.

(At a sign from Amneris, all withdraw.)

Nel rivederla, il dubbio atroce in me si
desta...
Il mistero fatal si squarci alfine!

Fu la sorte dell'armi a tuoi funesta,
Povera Aida! Il lutto che ti pesa sul cor teco
divido.
Io son l'amica tua...tutto da me tu avrai...
Vivrai felice!

When I see her again, fearful doubt is
awakened in me!
Let the fatal mystery at last be revealed!

(to Aida, with feigned affection)
The fate of war was deadly to your people.
Poor Aida! I share with you the burden in
your heart.
I am your friend. I will give you everything
and you will live happily!

Aida:
Felice esser poss'io lungi dal suol natio, qui
dove ignota m'è la sorte del padre e dei
fratelli?

Aida:
Can I be happy far from my homeland,
here where the fate of my father and
brothers is unknown to me?

Amneris:
Ben ti compagno! Pure hanno un confine
I mali di quaggiù.
Sanerà il tempo le angosce del tuo core,
e più che il tempo, un Dio possente.. amore!

Amneris:
I have compassion for you. I share your
grief but it will end.
Time will heal the anguish in your heart,
and more than time, a powerful god....love!

Aida:
(Amore, amore!
Gaudio, tormento, soave ebbrezza, ansia
crudel!
Ne' tuoi dolori la vita io sento, un tuo
sorriso mi schiude il ciel.)

Aida:
(Love, love!
Tormented joy, gentle sorrow, cruel
anxiety!
I feel life in your compassion, your smile
opens heaven.)

Amneris:
(Ah, quel pallore... quel turbamento
svelan l'arcana febbre d'amor.
D'interrogarla quasi ho sgomento,
divido l'ansie del suo terror)

Amneris: *(looking fixedly at Aida)*
(Ah! That pallor...that torment reveals the
mysterious secret of feverish love.
I'll question her and pretend to share the
anxiety of her torment)
(to Aida)

Ebben: qual nuovo fremito t'assai gentil
Aida?
I tuoi segreti svelami,
all'amor mio t'affida.
Tra i forti che pugnarono
della tua patria a danno.
Qualcuno... un dolce affanno
forse... a te in cor destò?

Aida:
Che parli?

Amneris:
A tutti barbara non si mostrò la sorte se in
campo il duce impavido cadde trafitto a morte.

Aida:
Che mai dicesti! Misera!

Amneris:
Sì... Radames da'tuoi fu spento...

Aida:
Misera!

Amneris:
E pianger puoi?

Aida:
Per sempre io piangerò!

Amneris:
Gli Dei t'han vendicata.

Aida:
Avversi sempre a me furo i Numi.

Amneris:
Trema! In cor ti lessi...
Tu l'ami...

Aida:
Io!

Amneris:
Non mentire!

Well: what new fears assault you, gentle
Aida?
Unveil your secrets, and confide in me
about love.
Among those brave men who fought so
valiantly for your country, is there someone
for whom sorrow has been awakened on
your heart?

Aida:
What did you say?

Amneris:
The fates are not so kind if a brave leader
falls to his death on the battelfied.

Aida:
What did you say? Misery!

Amneris:
Yes...Radames was killed....

Aida:
Misery!

Amneris:
And you weep?

Aida:
I will always weep!

Amneris:
The gods have been avenging.

Aida:
The furor of the gods was always against me.

Amneris:
Tremble! I read the secret in your heart...
You love him....

Aida:
I!

Amneris:
Don't lie!

Un detto ancora e il vero saprò.
Fissami in volto...io t'ingannava... Radames
vive!

Aida:
Vive! Ah, grazie, o Numi!

Amneris:
E ancor mentir tu speri?
Sì, tu l'ami! Ma l'amo anch'io,
intendi tu? Son tua rivale, figlia dei Faraoni.

Aida:
Mia rivale!
Ebben sia pure... Anch'io son tal.............

Ah! Che dissi mai? Pietà, perdono! Ah!

Pietà ti prenda del mio dolor.
È vero, io l'amo d'immenso amor.
Tu sei felice, tu sei possente,
io vivo solo per questo amor!

Amneris:
Trema, vil schiava! Spezza il tuo core;
Segnar tua morte può quest'amore;
Del tuo destino arbitra sono,
D'odio e vendetta le furie ho in cor.

Aida:
Tu sei felice, tu sei possente.
Io vivo solo per questo amor!
Pietà ti prenda del mio dolor!

Amneris:
Trema, vil schiava! Spezza il tuo core.
Del tuo destino arbitra sono.
D'odio e vendetta le furie ho in cor.

Coro:
Su! Del Nilo al sacro lido
sien barriera i nostri petti;
non echeggi che un sol grido:
guerra e morte allo stranier!

One more word and I will know the truth.
Look at me firmly...I have deceived you..
Radames lives!

Aida:
He lives! Ah, thanks to the gods!

Amneris:
And you still lie to me?
Yes. You love him! But I love him too.
Do you understand? I am your rival, a
daughter of the Pharaohs.

Aida:
Mi rival!
So be it. I am also a........................

(restraining herself)
Ah! What did I say? Mercy, pardon! Ah!

Have mercy on my grief.
It is true, I love him immensely.
You are happy, you are powerful,
I live only for that love!

Amneris:
Tremble, vile slave! Be heartbroken.
This love shall signal your death.
I judge your destiny.
I have vengeance and hate in my heart.

Aida:
You are happy, you are powerful.
I live only for that love!
Have mercy on my grief!

Amneris:
Tremble, vile slave! Be heartbroken.
I am the judge of your destiny.
I have hate and vengeance in my heart.

Chorus: *(from outside)*
Arise! From the sacred shores of the Nile,
our breasts will be a barrier.
Let there be but one cry:
war and death to the foreigner!

Amneris:
Alla pompa che s'appresta,
Meco, o schiava, assisterai;
Tu prostrata nella povere,
Io sul trono, accanto al Re.

Amneris:
The pomp of celebration approaches.
Come with me slave, and assist me.
Prostrate yourself on the dust.
I will be on the throne, next to the Pharaoh.

Aida:
Ah pietà! Che più mi resta?
Un deserto è la mia vita;
Viva e regna, il tuo furore io tra breve
placherò.
Quest'amore che t'irrita nella tomba io
spegnerò.

Aida:
Ah mercy! What more remains for me?
My life is a desert;.
life and reign, but your fury will soon be
appeased.
This love that irritates you will be extinguished in the tomb.

Amneris:
Vien, mi segui, apprenderai
se lottar tu puoi con me.

Amneris:
Come, follow me, you will learn to struggle
with me.

Aida:
Ah! pietà!
Quest'amor nella tomba io spegnerò.
Pietà! pietà!

Aida:
Ah! Mercy!
This love will be extinguished in the tomb.
Mercy! Mercy!

Coro:
Guerra e morte allo stranier!

Chorus:
War and death to the foreigner!

Amneris:
... e apprenderai se lottar tu puoi con me.

Amneris:
...and you will learn you cannot fight me.

Coro:
Guerra e morte allo stranier!

Chorus:
War and death to the foreigner!
(Amneris exits)

Aida:
Numi, pietà del mio martir,
speme non v'ha pel mio dolor!
Numi, pietà del mio soffrir!
Numi, pietà, pietà, pietà!

Aida:
Gods, have mercy on my suffering,
I have no hope from my sadness!
Gods, mercy on my suffering!
Gods, mercy, mercy, mercy!

ACT II - Scene 2

The entrance gates of the city of Thebes, before the temple of Ammon

Popolo:
Gloria all'Egitto, ad Iside che il sacro suol
protegge!
Al Re che il Delta regge inni festosi alziam!
Gloria! Gloria! Gloria! Gloria al Re!

People:
Glory to Egypt, and to Isis who protects our
sacred soil!
We raise hymns of praise to the Pharaoh
who rules the Delta!
Glory! Glory! Glory! Glory to the Pharaoh!

Donne:
S'intrecci il loto al lauro sul crin dei
vincitori!
Nembo gentil di fiori
stenda sull'armi un vel.
Danziam, fanciulle egizie,
le mistiche carole, come d'intorno al sole
Danzano gli astri in ciel!

Women:
Weave the lotus and the laurel for the
crown of the victors!
A gentle shower of flowers!
Spread a veil on the armies.
We dance, Egyptian daughters,
the mystic dance like the stars of heaven
around the sun!

Ramfis, Sacerdoti:
Della vittoria agl'arbitri supremi il guardo
ergete;
grazie agli Dei rendete nel fortunato dì.

Ramphis, Priests:
The supreme judges raise their eyes to the
victory.
Render thanks to the gods on this fortunate
day.

Popolo:
Come d'intorno al sole danzano gli astri in
ciel!
Inni festosi alziam al Re.

People:
Like the stars of heaven that dance around
the sun!
We raise hymns of praise to the Pharaoh..

Ramfis, Sacerdoti:
Grazie agli Dei rendete nel fortunato dì.

Ramphis, Priests:
Render thanks to the gods on this fortunate
day.

*The Egyptian troops file before the Pharaoh in chariots bearing their ensigns, sacred vases
and statues of the gods. Dancing girls carry the treasures of the vanquished, and lastly,
Radames appears, supported under a canopy borne by Officers.*

Grand March

Allegro maestoso

Popolo:
Vieni, o guerriero vindice,
Vieni a gioir con noi; sul passo degli eroi
I lauri, i fior versiam!
Gloria al guerrier, gloria!
Gloria all'Egitto, gloria!

People:
Come, o victorious warrior,
come and share our joy. In the path of the
heroes we shed flowers and laurels!
Glory to the warrior, glory!
Glory to Egypt, glory!

Ramfis, Sacerdoti:
Agli arbitri supremi il guardo ergete;
Grazie agli Dei rendete nel fortunato dì.

Ramphis, Priests:
The supreme judges raise their eyes to the
victory. Render thanks to the gods on this
fortunate day.

*(Pharaoh descends from the throne to
embrace Radames)*

Il Re:
Salvator della patria io ti saluto.
Vieni, e mia figlia di sua man ti porga il
serto trionfale.

Pharaoh:
Savior of our country, I salute you.
Come, and my daughter will place the
triumphal crown on you.

*(Radames kneels before Amneris who
places the crown on him)*

Ora, a me chiedi quanto più brami.
Nulla a te negato sarà in tal dì; lo giuro
per la corona mia, pei sacri Numi.

Now, ask of me your wish.
Nothing will be denied you; I swear it by
my crown and the sacred gods.

Radames:
Concedi in pria che innanzi a te sien tratti
i prigionier.

Radames:
First concede to let the prisoners come
forth before you.

*The Ethiopian prisoners are brought forward by Guards.
The last to appear is Amonasro, dressed as an Officer.*

Ramfis, Sacerdoti:
Grazie agli Dei rendete
nel fortunato dì.

Ramphis, Priests:
Render thanks to the gods on this fortunate
day.

Aida:
Che veggo!... Egli!... Mio padre!

Aida:
What do I see! Him! My father!

Tutti:
Suo padre!

All:
Her father!

Amneris:
In poter nostro!

Amneris:
In our power!

Aida:
Tu! Prigionier!

Amonasro:
Non mi tradir!

Il Re:
T'appressa...
Dunque tu sei?...

Amonasro:
Suo padre. Anch'io pugnai...
vinti noi fummo, morte invan cercai.
Quest'assisa ch'io vesto vi dica
che il mio Re, la mia patria ho difeso;
fu la sorte a nostr'armi nemica.
Tornò vano dei forti l'ardir.
Al mio pie nella polve disteso
giacque il Re da più colpi trafitto.
Se l'amor della patria è delitto
siam rei tutti, siam pronti a morir!

Aida: *(embracing her father)*
You! A prisoner!

Amonasro: *(whispering to Aida)*
Don't betray me!

Pharaoh: *(to Amonasro)*
Come nearer...
Who are you?

Amonasro:
Her father. I also fought....
I was defeated, I yearned for death in vain.
This uniform I wear may tell you
that I defended my country for my king;
victory was the destiny of our enemy armies.
The courage of the brave was in vain.
At my feet in the dust lay my king, pained
by many wounds,
If the love of country is a crime,
we are all criminals, all ready to die!

Ma tu, Re, tu signore possente,
A costoro ti volgi clemente;
Oggi noi siam percossi dal fato,
ma doman voi potria il fato colpir.

But you, Pharaoh, you powerful lord,
be merciful to these men.
Today we are struck by fate,
but tomorrow fate may strike you.

Aida:
Ma tu, Re, tu signore possente,
a costoro ti volgi clemente.

Aida:
But you, Pharaoh, you powerful lord,
be merciful to these men.

Schiave, Prigionieri:
Sì, dai Numi percossi noi siamo,
tua pietà, tua clemenza imploriamo.
Ah! Giammai di soffrir vi sia dato
ciò che in oggi n'è dato soffrir!

Slaves, Prisoners:
Yes, we were struck by the gods.
We implore your pity and mercy.
Ah! May you never have to suffer
the way we have had to suffer!

Amonasro:
Ah! Doman voi potria il fato colpir.

Amonasro:
Ah! Tomorrow fate may strike you.

Ramfis, Sacerdoti:
Struggi, o Re, queste ciurme feroci,
chiudi il core alle perfide voci;
fu dai Numi votati alla morte.
Or de'Numi si compia il voler!

Ramphis, Priests:
Oh Pharaoh, destroy these savage hordes,.
close your heart to their perfidious voices;
the gods doomed them to death.
Let the will of the gods be done!

Aida. Schiave, Prigionieri:
Pietà!

Aida, Slaves, Prisoners:
Pity!

Aida:
Ma tu, o Re, signor possente,
a costoro ti volgi clemente;
oggi noi siam percossi dal fato,
ma doman voi potria il fato colpir.

Aida:
But you, Pharaoh, you powerful lord,
be merciful to these men.
Today we are victims of fate,
but tomorrow fate may strike you.

Schiave, Prigionieri:
Sì, dai Numi percossi noi siamo,
tua pietà, tua clemenza imploriamo;
ah! Giammai di soffrir vi sia dato
ciò che in oggi n'è dato soffrir!

Slaves, Prisoners:
Yes, we were stricken by the gods.
We implore your pity and mercy.
Ah! May you never have to suffer
the way we have had to suffer!

Amonasro:
Ah! doman voi potria il fato colpir.

Amonasro:
Ah! Tomorrow fate may strike you.

Ramfis, Sacerdoti:
Struggi, o Re, queste ciurme feroci,
Chiudi il core alle perfide voci;
fu dai Numi votati alla morte,
or de' Numi si compia il voler!

Ramphis, Priests:
Oh Pharaoh, destroy these savage hordes.
Close your heart to their perfidious voices.
The gods doomed them to death.
Let the will of the gods be done!

Aida, Schiave, Prigionieri:
Pietà!

Aida, Slaves, Prisoners:
Mercy!

Aida:
Ma tu, o Re, signor possente,
a costoro ti mostra clemente.

Aida:
But you, Pharaoh, you powerful lord,
be merciful to these men.

Amneris:
(Quali sguardi sovr'essa ha rivolti!
Di qual fiamma balenano i volti!)

Amneris:
(What glances he makes toward her!
Their faces are aflame!)

Il Re:
Or che fausti ne arridon gli eventi
a costoro mostriaci clementi.

Pharaoh:
Now that events smile favorably upon us,
let us show mercy to these people.

Schiave, Prigionieri:
Tua pietade, tua clemenza imploriamo,
Ah, pietà! pietà!

Slaves, Prisoners:
We implore your pity and mercy,
Ah! Mercy! Mercy!

Popolo:
Sacerdoti, gli sdegni placate, l'umil prece
ascoltate.

People:
Priests, placate your scorn and heed their
humble pleas.

Ramfis, Sacerdoti:
A morte! A morte! A morte!
O Re, struggi queste ciurme.

Ramphis, Priests:
Death! Death! Death!
Oh Pharaoh, suppress this trickery.

Amonasro:
Oggi noi siam percossi dal fato,
voi doman potria il fato colpir.

Amonasro:
Today we are victims of fate,
tomorrow fate may strike you.

Radames:
(Il dolor che in quel volto favella
al mio sguardo la rende più bella;
ogni stilla del pianto adorato
nel mio petto ravviva l'amor)

Radames: *(looking at Aida)*
(The sorrow in her face makes her more
beautiful to me.
Every drop of her beloved tears revives
love in my breast.)

Amneris:
(Quali sguardi sovr'essa ha rivolti!
Di qual fiamma balenano i volti!
Ed io sola, avvilita, reietta?
La vendetta mi rugge nel cor.)

Amneris:
(What glances he makes toward her!
Their faces are aflame!)
And I, reviled, rejected?
Vengeance inflames my heart.)

Amonasro:
Tua pietà, tua clemenze imploriamo......

Amonasro:
We implore you, pity, mercy......

Il Re:
Or che fausti ne arridon gli eventi
a costoro mostriaci clementi;
la pietà sale ai Numi gradita
E rafferma de'prenci il poter.

Pharaoh:
Now that events smile favorably upon us
let us show mercy to these people.
The grateful gods are merciful and
empower their princes.

Aida:
Tua pietà imploro...
Oggi noi siam percossi,
Doman voi potria il fato colpir.

Aida:
I implore your mercy....
Today we are struck by fate.
Tomorrow fate may strike you.

Schiave, Prigionieri:
Pietà, pietà, ah pietà!
Tua clemenza imploriam.
Tua pietade, tua clemenza invochiamo.

Slaves, Prisoners:
Mercy, mercy, ah mercy!
We implore your mercy.
We invoke your mercy and clemency.

Popolo:
Sacerdoti, gli sdegni placate.
L'umil prece de' vinti ascoltate; pietà!

People:
Priests, placate your scorn and heed their
humble pleas; mercy!

Ramfis, Sacerdoti:
Si compisca dei Numi il voler!
Struggi, o Re, queste ciurme feroci.
Fu dai Numi votati alla morte,
si compisca de' Numi il voler!

Ramphis, Priests:
Let the will of the gods be done!
Oh Pharaoh destroy these savage hordes.
The gods doomed them to death.
Let the will of the gods be done!

Aida:
Ma tu, o Re, tu signore possente....

Aida:
But you, o Pharaoh, powerful lord....

Radames:
(Il dolor la rende più bella....)

Radames:
(The sorrow in her face makes her more beautiful.)

Amonasro:
Ma tu, o Re, tu signore possente......

Amonasro:
But you, o Pharaoh, powerful lord....

Il Re:
La pietà sale ai Numi gradita......

Pharaoh:
The grateful gods have mercy.....

Schiave, Prigionieri:
Sì, dai Numi percossi noi siamo......

Slaves, Prisoners:
Yes, we were stricken by the gods....

Ramfis, Sacerdoti:
Struggi, o Re, queste ciurme feroci.....

Ramphis, Priests:
Oh Pharaoh, destroy these savage hordes....

Popolo:
E tu, o Re possente, tu forte, a clemenza
dischiudi il pensier.

People:
And you, o powerful Pharaoh, you are
strong, let mercy flow from your thoughts.

Amneris:
(Ed io sola, avvilita, ecc)

Amneris:
(And I vilified, rejected.....)

Radames::
O Re: pei sacri Numi,
per lo splendor della tua corona,
compier giurasti il voto mio.

Radames:
Oh Pharaoh, by the sacred gods,
by the glory of your crown,
you swore to fulfill my vow.

Il Re:
Giurai.

Pharaoh:
I swore.

Radames:
Ebbene: a te pei prigionieri Etiopi
Vita domando e libertà.

Radames:
Then I demand life and liberty for the
Ethiopian prisoners.

Amneris:
(Per tutti!)

Sacerdoti:
Morte ai nemici della patria!

Popolo:
Grazia per gli infelici!

Ramfis:
Ascolta o Re. Tu pure,
giovine eroe, saggio consiglio ascolta.
Son nemici e prodi sono;
la vendetta hanno nel cor,
fatti audaci dal perdono
correranno all'armi ancor!

Radames:
Spento Amonasro, il re guerrier, non resta
speranza ai vinti.

Ramfis:
Almeno, arra di pace e securtà, fra noi
resti col padre Aida.

Il Re:
Al tuo consiglio io cedo.
Di securtà, di pace un miglior pegno
or io vo' darvi:
Radamès, la patria tutto a te deve.
d'Amneris la mano premio ti sia.
Sovra l'Egitto un giorno con essa regnerai.

Amneris:
(Venga la schiava, venga a rapirmi l'amor
mio... se l'osa!)

Il Re, Popolo:
Gloria all'Egitto, ad Iside che il sacro suol
difende.
S'intrecci il loto al lauro sul crin del vincitor!

Schiave, Prigionieri:
Gloria al clemente Egizio
che i nostri ceppi ha sciolto.
che ci ridona ai liberi
solchi del patrio suol!

Amneris:
(For all!)

Priests:
Death to the enemies of our country!

People:
Grace for the unhappy!

Ramphis:
Listen o Pharaoh. Young hero listen to the
following wise counsel.
They are an enemy with pride and
with vengeance in their heart.
If emboldened by a pardon they will take
arms again!

Radames:
Their warrior king, Amonasro, is dead, and
no hope remains for the vanquished.

Ramphis:
At least as security and peace, let Aida and
her father remain. The rest can go free.

Pharaoh:
I yield to your counsel.
For the security of our country, I will give
you a better pledge.
Radames, I give you the country and the
hand of Amneris as your reward.
One day, with her, you will rule over Egypt.

Amneris:
(Now let the slave come... let her dare to
come to take my love from me!)

Pharaoh, People:
Glory to Egypt, and to Isis who protects our
sacred soil!
On the head of the victors place the laurels!

Slaves, Prisoners:
Glory to merciful Egypt
who has loosened our shackles,
who restores us to freedom and the path to
our native soil!

Ramfis, Sacerdoti:
Inni leviamo ad Iside che il sacro suol
difende!
Preghiam che i fati arridano
fausti alla patria ognor.

Aida:
(Qual speme omai più restami?
A lui la gloria, il trono, a me l'oblio... le
lacrime d'un disperato amor.)

Radames:
(Davverso Nume il folgore sul capo mio
discende.
Ah no! D'Egitto il soglio son val d'Aida il
cor.)

Amneris:
(Dall'inatteso giublio inebriata io sono;
tutti in un dì si compiono i sogni del mio
cor.)

Ramfis:
Preghiam che i fati arridano fausti alla
patria ognor.

Il Re, Popolo:
Gloria... ad Iside!

Amonasro:
Fa cor: della tua patria I lieti eventi aspetta;
Per noi della vendetta già prossimo è
l'albor.

Radames:
(Qual inattesa folgore
su capo mio discende! Ah!
Ah no! D'Egitto il trono non val d'Aida il
cor.
... d'Egitto il suol non val d'Aida il cor.
... d'Egitto il soglio non val d'Aida il cor.)

Amneris:
(Tutte in un dì si compiono
le gioie del mio cor.

Ramphis, Priests:
We raise hymns to Isis who has defended
our sacred soil!
We pray that the fates will ever smile
favorably on our country.

Aida:
(What hope remains for me?)
He has glory and the throne. For me there is
only oblivion, tears, and a hopeless love.)

Radames:
(The thunder of the avenging gods
descends on my head.
Ah no! The throne of Egypt is not worth
losing Aida's heart.)

Amneris:
(I am intoxicated by this unexpected joy.
The dreams in my heart are fulfilled in this
one day!)

Ramphis:
We pray that the fates will ever smile
favorably on our country.

Pharaoh, People:
Glory....to Isis!

Amonasro: *(to Aida)*
Take heart: your country anticipates
propitious.
For us the dawn of vengeance is already
near.

Radames:
(What unexpected thunder descends on my
head! Ah!
Ah no! The throne of Egypt is not worth
losing Aida's heart...
..the soil of Egypt is not worth losing Aida's
heart.)

Amneris:
(All in one day the joy in my heart is
fulfilled.

Ah! Dall'inatteso guadio
inebriata io sono)

Ah! I am intoxicated by this unexpected
joy.)

Amonasro:
Fa cor: la tua patria
i lieti eventi aspetta........

Amonasro:
Take heart: your country anticipates
propitious events...........

Il Re, Popolo:
Gloria, all'Egitto e ad Iside.........

Pharaoh, People:
Glory to Egypt and Isis...........

Ramfis, Sacerdoti:
Inni leviamo ad Iside.............

Ramphis, Priests:
We raise our prayers to Isis.......

Aida::
(A me l'oblio, le lacrime.
Ah! Qual speme omai più restami?
A lui la gloria, il trono, a me l'oblio, le
lacrime d'un disperato amor)

Aida:
(For me oblivion and tears.
Ah! What hope remains for me?
He has glory and the throne. For me there is
only despair, tears, and a hopeless love.)

Schiave, Prigionieri:
Gloria al clemente Egizio.....

Slaves, Prisoners:
Glory to merciful Egypt...........

ACT III

The Banks of the Nile. The Temple of Isis is half concealed among the foliage.
It is an evening with starlight and bright moonlight.

Sacerditesse, Sacerdoti:
O tu che sei d'Osiride.
Madre immortale e sposa,
Diva che i casti palpiti desti agli umani in cor.
Soccorri a noi pietosa, madre d'immenso
amor.

Priestesses, Priests:
O you Osiris, immortal mother and spouse.
Goddess who stirs the beatings of human
hearts.
Mother of immense love help us and be
merciful and compassionate.

Amneris approaches the shore by boat, accompanied by Ramphis,
closely veiled women, and Guards.

Ramfis:
Vieni d'Iside al tempio: alla vigilia
delle tue nozze, invoca della Diva il favore.
Iside legge de' mortali nel core; ogni
mistero degli umani a lei è noto.

Ramphis: *(to Amneris)*
Come to the temple of Isis on the vigil of
your wedding, and invoke the Goddess's
blessings. Isis reads the hearts of mortals;
every human mystery is known to her.

Amneris:
Sì! Io pregherò che Radamès mi doni
tutto il suo cor, come il mio cor a lui
sacro è per sempre.

Amneris:
Yes, I will pray that Radames will give me
his whole heart, as I will give him my
consecrated heart forever.

Ramfis:
Andiamo.
Pregherai fino all'alba; io sarò teco.

Ramphis:
Let us go.
Pray until dawn; I will be with you.
(they enter the temple)

Sacerdotesse, Sacerdoti:
Soccorri a noi pietosa,
Madre d'immenso amor.

Priestesses, Priests:
Mother of immense love help us and be
merciful and compassionate.

Aida:
Qui Radamès verrà!
Che vorrà dirmi?
Io tremo... Ah! Se tu vieni
a recarmi, o crudel, l'ultimo addio.
Del Nilo i cupi vortici
mi daran tomba... e pace forse, e oblio.

Aida: *(Aida enters cautiously)*
Radames will come here!
What will he say to me?
I tremble. Ah! You come to give me a cruel,
ultimate farewell.
The deep Nile will be my tomb, and
perhaps peace and eternal oblivion.

Andante mosso

O cieli az - zur - ri, o dol - ci au - re na - ti - ve,

O patria mia, mai più ti revedrò!
O cieli azzurri, o dolci aure native,
dove sereno il nido mattin brillò,
O verdi colli, o profumate rive.
O patria mia, mai più ti revedrò!
O fresche valli, o queto asil beato,
che un dì promesso dall'amor mi fu.
Or che d'amore il sogno è dileguato,
o patria mia, non ti vedrò mai più!

Oh my country, I will never see you again!
Oh beautiful blue skies, the native soft air,
where my life was calm and peaceful.
Oh verdant hills, oh perfumed waters,
Oh my country, I will never see you again!
Oh fresh valleys, oh quiet dwellings,
It bore the promises of love,
and now that hope is vanished.
O my country, I will never see you again!

Amonasro appears

Ciel! mio padre!

Heavens! my father!

Amonasro:
A te grave cagion m'adduce, Aida.....
nulla sfugge al mio sguardo.
D'amor ti struggi per Radamès...
ei t'ama... qui lo attendi.
Dei Faraon la figlia è tua rivale...
razza infame, aborrita e a noi fatale!

Amonasro:
A grave cause leads me to you, Aida...
Nothing escapes my sight.
You destroy yourself with your love for
Radames....you await him here.
The Pharaoh's daughter is your rival...
Infamous race, abhorred and fatal to us!

Aida:
E in suo potere io sto! Io, d'Amonasro
figlia!

Aida:
And I am in their power, the daughter of
Amonasro!

Amonasro:
In poter di lei! No!... se lo brami
la possente rival tu vincerai,
e patria, e trono, e amor, tutto tu avrai.

Amonasro:
In her power! No!...if you wish you could
defeat that powerful rival, and country,
throne, and love, will be yours.

Allegro giusto

Ri - ve   drai   le for - es - te imbal - sa - ma - te,

Rivedrai le foreste imbalsamate, le fresche
valli, i nostri tempi d'or.

You will again see our balmy forests, the
fresh valleys, and our golden temples.

Aida:
Rivedrò le foreste imbalsamate, le fresche
valli, i nostri tempi d'or.

Aida:
I will see our balmy forests, fresh valleys,
and our temples of gold!

Amonasro:
Sposa felice a lui che amasti tanto,
tripudi immensi ivi potrai gioir.

Amonasro:
And be the happy bride of the man you
love so much, and be immensely happy.

Aida:
Un giorno solo di si dolce incanto,
un'ora, un'ora di tal gioia, e poi morir!

Aida:
Just one day of such enchantment,
one hour, one hour of joy before I die!

Amonasro:
Pur rammenti che a noi l'Egizio immite,
le case, i tempi, e l'are profanò.
Trasse in ceppi le vergini rapite;
madri, vecchi, fanciulli ei trucidò.

Amonasro:
But remember that the merciless Egyptians
profaned our houses and temples,
put our virgins in chains and ravished them,
slew mothers, elderly, and children.

Aida:
Ah! ben rammento quegl'infausti giorni!
Rammento i lutti che il mio cor soffrì.
Deh! Fate, o Numi, che per soi ritorni
l'alba invocata de'sereni dì.

Aida:
Ah! I remember those unhappy days well!
I remember the grief I suffered.
Ah! Fate, oh gods, let us return to the
longed for dawn of peaceful days.

Amonasro:
Non fia che tardi. In armi ora si desta.
Il popol nostro, tutto è pronto già.
Vittoria avrem... Solo a saper mi resta,
qual sentier il nemico seguirà.

Amonasro:
Don't delay. Our people are already in
arms, and all is ready.
We will be victorious. It only remains for me to
know the path the enemy will follow.

Aida:
Chi scoprirlo potria? Chi mai?

Aida:
Who will be able to discover it? Who?

Amonasro::
Tu stessa!

Amonasro:
You alone!

Aida:
Io!

Aida:
I!

Amonasro:
Radamès so che qui attendi... ei t'ama...
Ei conduce gli Egizi... Intendi?...

Amonasro:
Radames will come here soon.. He loves
you. He leads the Egyptians. Understand?

Aida:
Orrore!
Che mi consigli tu? No! No! Giammai!

Aida:
Horror!
What are you asking me to do? No! No! Never!

Amonasro:
Su, dunque! Sorgete Egizie coorti!
Col fuoco struggete le nostre città.
Spargete il terrore, le stragi, la morte...
Al vostro fuore più freno non v'ha.

Amonasro: *(impetuously and savagely)*
Up, then! Arise Egyptian legions!
Destroy our cities with fire.
Spread terror, carnage, and death...
There is no resistance to your fury.

Aida:
Ah padre! Padre!...

Aida:
Ah father! Father!

Amonasro:
Mia figlia ti chiami!
Aida:
Pietà! Pietà! Pietà!

Amonasro:
You call yourself my daughter?
Aida:
Mercy! Mercy! Mercy!

Amonasro:
Flutti di sangue scorrono sulle città dei
vinti.

Amonasro:
Rivers of blood will pour on the vanquished cities.

Vedi? Dai negri vortici si levano gli estinti,
ti additan essi e gridano:
"Per te la patria muor!"

Do you see? From the black gulfs the dead
rise, and point to you and cry:
"Because of you your country dies."

Aida:
Pietà! Pietà, padre, pietà!

Aida:
Mercy! Mercy, father, mercy!

Amonasro:
Una larva orribile
fra l'ombre a noi s'affaccia.
Trema! Le scarne braccia sul capo tuo levò...
Tua madre ell'è ravvisala.
Ti maledice.

Amonasro:
A horrible ghost approaches from out of the
shadows.
Tremble! The fleshless arms are raised.
It is your mother, recognize her.
She curses you.

Aida:
Ah no! Ah no!
Padre, pietà! Pietà!

Aida:
Ah no! Ah no!
Mercy, mercy! Mercy!

Amonasro:
Non sei mia figlia!
Dei Faraoni tu sei la schiava!

Amonasro:
You are not my daughter!
You are a slave of the Pharaohs!

Aida:
Padre, a costoro schiava non sono...
Non maledirmi... non imprecarmi.
Ancor tua figlia potrai chiamarmi,
della mia patria degna sarò.

Aida:
Father, I am not their slave...
Don't curse me..don't reproach me,
You will call me your daughter again.
I will be worthy of my country.

Amonasro:
Pensa che un popolo, vinto, straziato,
per te soltanto risorger può...

Amonasro:
Think of the people, defeated, torn,
who can only rise through you....

Aida:
O patria! O patria, quanto mi costi!

Aida:
Oh my country! Oh my country, how much
you cost me!

Amonasro:
Coraggia! Ei giunge... là tutto udrò.

Amonasro:
Courage! He arrives.....there I will hear all.
(Conceals himself among the palm trees)

Allegro giusto

Pur ti   ri - veg   -   go, mia dol-ce A - i   -   da,

Radames:
Pur ti riveggo, mia dolce Aida...

Aida:
T'arresta, vanne... che speri ancor?

Radames:
A te d'appresso l'amor mi guida.

Aida:
Te i riti attendono d'un altro amor.
D'Amneris sposo...

Radames:
Che parli mai?
Te sola, Aida, te deggia amar.
Gli Dei m'ascoltano, tu mia sarai.

Aida:
D'uno spergiuro non ti macchiar!
Prode t'amai, non t'amerei spergiuro.

Radames:
Dell'amor mio dubiti, Aida?

Aida:
E come speri sottrarti d'Amneris ai vezzi,
del Re al voler, del tuo popolo ai voti,
dei Sacerdoti all'ira?

Radames:
Odimi, Aida.
Nel fiero anelito di nuova guerra il suolo
Etiope si ridestò;
i tuoi già invadono la nostra terra,
io degli Egizi duce sarò.
Fra il suon, fra i plausi della vittoria,
al Re mi prostro.
Gli svelo il cor.
Sarai tu il serto della mia gloria,
vivrem beati d'eterno amore.

Aida:
Nè d'Amneris paventi il vindice furor?
La sua vendetta come folgor tremenda,
cadrà su me, sul padre mio, su tutti.

Radames:
To see you again, my sweet Aida...

Aida:
Stop! Go away...what more do you want?

Radames:
Love has guided me to you.

Aida:
The rites of another love awaits you.
You are Amneris's spouse.

Radames:
What did you say?
It is you alone, Aida, whom I love.
The gods have listened, and you will be mine.

Aida:
Do not stain yourself by lying!
I loved you proudly, and swore my love.

Radames:
Do you doubt my love, Aida?

Aida:
How do you hope to free yourself from the
love of Amneris, from the King's will, from
the vows of your people, and from the
wrath of the Priests?

Radames:
Listen to me, Aida.
Ethiopia has awakened with the fierce
yearning for a new war.
Your people already invade our land, and
I will be the Egyptian leader.
Amid the fame and the applause of victory,
I will prostrate myself before the King.
I will unveil my heart.
You shall be the reward for my glory, and
we will live blessed by eternal love.

Aida:
Don't you fear Amneris's vindictive fury?
Her revenge, like a dreadful thunderbolt,
will fall on me, my father, on every one.

Radames:
Io vi difendo.

Radames:
I will defend you.

Aida:
Invan, tu nol potresti.
Pur... se tu m'ami... ancor s'apre una via
di scampo a noi...

Aida:
In vain, you will not be able to.
But...if you love me..there is yet a way of
escape open to us...

Radames:
Quale?

Radames:
Which?

Aida:
Fuggir...

Aida:
To flee!

Radames
Fuggire!

Radames:
To flee!

Aida:
Fuggiam gli ardori inospiti
di queste lande ignude.
Una novella patria al nostro amor si
schiude.

Aida:
We'll flee and leave this bare and blighted
desert,
A new country where our love will be united.

Andantino

Là   tra   fo-re - ste   ver - gi-ni,   di   fio - ri   pro-fu - ma   -   te,

Là... tra foreste vergini di fiori profumate,
in estasi beate la terra scorderem.

There...among the virgin forests and
fragrant flowers, in blessed ecstasy we'll
forget this land.

Radames:
Sovra una terra estrania teco fuggir dovrei!
Abbandonar la patria, l'are dei nostri Dei!
Il suol dov'io raccolsi di gloria i primi allori.
Il ciel dei nostri amori come scordar
potrem?

Radames:
I should flee with you to a faraway land!
Abandon my country where I was
victorious, and the altars of our gods.
How can we forget the skies that ignited
our love?

Aida:
Là... tra foreste vergini.....

Aida:
There...among the virgin forests.....

Radames:
Il ciel dei nostri amori come scordar
potrem?

Radames:
How can we forget the skies that ignited
our love?

Aida:
Sotto il mio ciel, più libero l'amor ne fia
concesso;
ivi nel tempio istesso gli stessi Numi
avrem.
Fuggiam, fuggiam!.

Radames:
Abbandonar la patria l'are dei nostri Dei!
Il ciel dei nostri amori come scordar
potrem?

Radames::
Aida!

Aida::
Tu non m'ami... Va!

Radames:
Non t'amo?

Aida:
Va!

Radames:
Mortal giammai né Dio
arse d'amor al par del mio possente.

Aida:
Va... va... t'attende all'ara Amneris...

Radames:
No! Giammai!

Aida:
Giammai, dicesti?
Allor piombi la scure
su me, sul padre mio...

Radames:
Ah no! Fuggiamo!
Sì, fuggiam da queste mura,
al deserto insiem fuggiamo.
Qui sol regna la sventura.
Là si schiude un ciel d'amor,
i deserti interminati a noi tal amo saranno.

Aida:
Under my skies, our love is more free and
without concessions,
We'll find the same gods in those same
temples. We will have gods.
Let us flee, flee!.

Radames:
Abandon my country, the altars of our gods.
How can we forget the skies that ignited
our love?

Radames: *(hesitating)*
Aida!

Aida:
You do not love me....Go!

Radames:
I don't love you?

Aida:
Go!

Radames:
There was never a mortal nor god who
burned with such powerful love.

Aida:
Go...go...Amneris awaits you at the altar..

Radames:
No! Never!

Aida:
You said never?
Then the axe will fall on me and on my
father...

Radames:
Ah no! Let us flee!
Yes. we'll flee from these walls,
we'll flee to the desert together.
Here only misfortune reigns.
There the heavens open for our love,
the boundless deserts will be nuptial couch.

Su noi gli astri brilleranno di più limpido
fulgor.

Aida:
Nella terra avventurata de' miei padri, il ciel
ne attende.
Ivi l'aura è imbalsamata, ivi il suolo è aromi
e fior.
Fresche valli e verdi prati a noi tal amo
saranno.
Su noi gli astri brilleranno
di più limpido fulgor.

Aida e Radames:
Vieni meco, insiem fuggiamo
Questa terra di dolore.
Vieni meco t'amo, t'amo!
A noi duce fia l'amor.

Aida:
Ma dimmi; per qual via eviterem le schiere
degli armati?

Radames:
Il sentier scelto dai nostri a piombar sul
nemico fia deserto fino a domani.

Aida:
E quel sentier?

Radames:
Le gole di Napata...

Amonasro:
Di Napata le gole!
Ivi saranno i miei.

Radames:
Oh! Chi ci ascolta?

Amonasro:
D'Aida il padre e degli Etiopi il Re.

Radames:
Tu!... Amonasro! Tu! Il Re?...

Upon us the stars will shine with more
limpid brilliance.

Aida:
Heaven awaits us in the adventurous land
of my father.
There the air is perfumed, and the ground
is fragrant with the aroma of flowers.
Fresh valleys and verdant fields shall be our
nuptial couch.
The stars will shine upon us with more
limpid brilliance.

Aida and Radames:
Come with me, together we escape this
land of sadness.
Come with me, I love you, I love you!
Let love be our leader!
(They go rapidly aside)

Aida:
But tell me, by what road shall we take to
avoid the armies?

Radames:
The path chosen by our troops to ambush
the enemy will be deserted until tomorrow.

Aida:
And that path?

Radames:
The Napata gorges..
(Amonasro comes forward)
Amonasro:
The Napata gorges!
There my people shall be!

Radames:
Oh! Who overhears us?

Amonasro:
Aida's father and King of Ethiopia.

Radames:
You! Amonasro! You! The King?

Numi! Che dissi?
No! Nnon è ver! No! Sogno! Delirio è
questo...

Aida:
Ah no! Ti calma, ascoltami...

Amonasro:
A te l'amor d'Aida un soglio innalzerà!.

Aida:
All'amor mio t'affida.

Radames:
Io son disonorato!
Per te tradii la patria!

Aida:
Ti calma!

Amonasro:
No: tu non sei colpevole, era voler del fato.

Radames:
Io son disonorato!

Aida:
Ah no!

Amonasro:
No!

Radames:
Per te tradii la patria!

Amonasro:
No: tu non sei colpevole.

Aida:
Ti calma...

Amonasro:
Vien: oltre il Nil ne attendono i prodi a noi
devoti.
Là del tuo core i voti coronerà l'amor.

Vieni, vieni, vieni.

Gods! What did I say?
No! It can't be true! No! A dream! This is
delirium..

Aida:
Ah no! Calm yourself and listen to me.

Amonasro:
Aida's love shall raise you to a throne!

Aida:
Trust yourself in our love.

Radames:
I am dishonored!
For you I betrayed my country!

Aida:
Calm yourself!

Amonasro:
No: you are not guilty, it was the will of fate.

Radames:
I am dishonored!

Aida:
Ah no!

Amonasro
No!

Radames:
For you I betrayed my country!

Amonasro:
No! You are not guilty.

Aida:
Calm yourself...

Amonasro:
Come! Other proud, devoted and brave
men await us beyond the Nile.
There the vows of your heart shall be
crowned with love.
Come, come, come.

Amneris, Ramphis, Priests and Guards emerge from the temple.

Amneris:
Traditor!

Aida:
La mia rival!

Amonasro:

L'opra mia a strugger vieni!
Muori!...

Radames:
Arresta, insano!...

Amonasro:
O rabbia!

Ramfis:
Guardie, olà!

Radames:
Presto! Fuggite!

Amonasro:
Vieni, o figlia!

Ramfis:
L'inseguite!

Radames:
Sacerdote, io resto a te.

Amneris:
Traitor!

Aida:
My rival!

Amonasro:
(rushing upon Amneris with a dagger)
You come to destroy my work!
Die!

Radames: *(interposing himself)*
Stop, madman!

Amonasro:
Oh fury!

Ramphis:
Guards, here!

Radames: *(to Aida and Amonasro)*
Quickly. Flee!

Amonasro: *(taking Aida with him)*
Come, oh daughter!

Ramphis: *(to the Guards)*
Follow them!

Radames: *(to Ramphis)*
Priest! I remain with you.

ACT IV - Scene 1

A Hall in the King's Palace. There is a large gate which opens on the subterranean hall of judgment; a passage leads to the prison of Radames.

Amneris:
L'aborrita rivale a me sfuggia...
Dai Sacerdoti Radamès attende
Dei traditor la pena.
Traditore egli non è...
Pur rivelò di guerra l'alto segreto...
egli fuggir volea...con lei fuggire... traditori
tutti!
A morte! A morte!... O! Che mai parlo? Io
l'amo, Io l'amo sempre...
Disperato, insano è quest'amor che la mia
vita strugge.
O! S'ei potesse amarmi!
Vorrei salvarlo. E come? Si tenti!
Guardie: Radamès qui venga.

Amneris:
Già i Sacerdoti adunansi
arbitri del tuo fato.
Pur dell'accusa orribile scolpati ancor t'è
dato;
Ti scolpa e la tua grazia io pregherò dal
trono, e nunzia di perdono, si vita te sarò.

Radames:
Di mie discolpe i giudici mai non urdan
l'accento.
Dinanzi ai Numi, agl'uomini, né vil, né reo
mi sento.
Profferse il labbro incauto fatal segreto, è
vero, ma puro il mio pensiero e l'onor mio
restò.

Amneris:
Salvati dunque e scolpati.

Radames:
No.

Amneris: *(sadly before the gate)*
My abhorred rival escapes me...
Radames awaits the Priests and the
punishment of a traitor.
He is not a traitor..
But then he revealed a high secret
he wished to flee...with her...they are all
traitors!
To death! To death!..Oh! What did I say?
I love him, I will always love him.
This love is desperate, insane, and destroys
my life.
Oh! If he could love me!
I would save him. And how? I will try!
Guards: Bring Radames before me.

(Radames is brought forward)
Amneris:
The Priests have already gathered to judge
your fate.
Exculpate yourself of this horrible
accusation.
Exculpate yourself and I will beg for grace
from the throne, and I will be a messenger
of pardon and life for you.

Radames:
The judges will never hear excuses from
my voice;
I feel neither vile nor guilt before men and
the gods.   .
It is true that my incautious lips uttered the
fatal secret, but my thoughts are pure and
my honor remains.

Amneris:
Then save and exculpate yourself.

Radames:
No.

Amneris:
Tu morrai.

Amneris:
You will die.

Radames:
La vita aborro; d'ogni gaudio la fante inaridita.
Svanita ogni speranza, sol bramo di morir.

Radames:
I abhor life, its joys and happiness are lost,
Every hope is lost and I only yearn to die.

Amneris:
Morire! Ah! Tu dei vivere!
Sì, all'amor mio vivrai;
Per te le angosce orribili di morte io già provai;
T'amai... soffersi tanto...
Vegliai le notti in pianto...
e patria, e trono, e vita, tutto darei per te.

Amneris:
To die! Ah! You must live!
Yes, you will live for my love;
I have undergone dreadful anguish in my love for you.
I loved you...suffered so much..
I watched the nights in tears.. I would give all for you, country, throne, and life.

Radames:
Per essa anch'io la patria
e l'onor mio tradia...

Radames:
For her, I betrayed my country and my honor.....

Amneris:
Di lei non più!

Amneris:
She is no more!

Radames:
L'infamia m'attende e vuoi ch'io viva?
Misero appien mi festi, Aida a me togliesti,
Spenta l'hai forse e in dono offri la vita a me?

Radames:
Infamy awaits me, and you want me to live?
You have taken Aida from me and made me utterly miserable. Perhaps you killed her, and as a gift you offer me life?

Amneris:
Io, di sua morte origine!
No! Vive Aida!

Amneris:
I the cause of her death?
No! Aida lives!

Radames:
Vive!

Radames:
She lives!

Amneris:
Nei disperato anelito dell'orde fuggitive
sol cadde il padre.

Amneris:
During the desperate struggle of the fugitives only her father was slain.

Radames:
Ed ella?

Radames:
And she?

Amneris:
Sparve, né più novella s'ebbe...

Amneris:
She disappeared, and we have no more news.

Radames:
Gli Dei l'adducano salva alle patrie mura,
e ignori la sventura si chi per lei morrà!

Radames:
May the gods lead her to safety and her
native walls, ignorant of the misfortune of
the man who died for her.

Amneris:
Ma, s'io ti salvo, giurami che più non la
vedrai.

Amneris:
But, if I save you, swear to me that you will
never see her again.

Radames:
Nol posso!

Radames:
I cannot!

Amneris:
A lei rinunzia
per sempre... e tu vivrai!

Amneris:
Renounce her forever........
and you will live!

Radames:
Nol posso!

Radames:
I cannot!

Amneris:
Ancor una volta. A lei rinunzia.

Amneris:
Again, renounce her.

Radames:
È vano.

Radames:
It is in vain.

Amneris:
Morir vuoi dunque, insano?

Amneris:
Are you Insane, you want to die?

Radames:
Pronto a morir son già!

Radames:
I am already ready to die!

Amneris:
Chi ti salva, sciagurato, dalla sorte che
t'aspetta?
In furore hai tu cangiato un amor ch'egual
non ha.
De' miei pianti la vendetta ora il ciel si
compirà.

Amneris:
Who will save you, o wretch, from the fate
that awaits you?
In a fury you have changed a love that has
no equal.
Heaven will now exact revenge for my
tears.

Radames:
È la morte un ben supremo.
Se per lei morir m'e dato nel subir
l'estremo fato gaudi immensi il cor avrà.
L'ira umana più non temo,
Temo sol la tua pietà.

Radames:
Death is a supreme blessing.
If I am to die for her, my heart will feel the
greatest joy.
I fear human anger no more,
I only fear your pity.

Amneris:
Ah! Chi ti salva?
De' miei pianti la vendetta or dal ciel si
compirà.

Amneris:
Ah! Who will save you?
Heaven will now exact revenge for my
tears.

Radames leaves under guard.

Amneris:
Ohimè! Morir mi sento! O! Chi lo salva?
E in poter di costoro
io stessa lo gettai! Ora a te impreco.
Atroce gelosia, che la sua morte
e il lutto eterno del mio cor segnasti!

Amneris: *(falls despairingly)*
Alas! I feel myself dying!
Oh! Who will save him?
I myself threw him into their power.
Atrocious jealousy, his death will be the
eternal grief in my heartt!

She turns and sees the Priests, who enter the subterranean hall.

Ecco i fatali, gl'inesorati ministri di morte!
O! Ch'io non vegga quelle bianche larve!
E in poter di costoro io stessa lo gettai!

Here are the fatal inexorable ministers of death!
Oh! That I may not see those white ghosts!
And I myself threw him into their power!

Ramfis, Sacerdoti:
Spirito del Nume, sovra noi discendi!
Ne avviva al raggio dell'eterna luce;
Pel labbro nostro tua giustizia apprendi.

Ramphis, Priests: *(from the hall)*
Spirit of the gods descend upon us!
Awaken us to the ray of your eternal light:
Make your justice known through our lips.

Amneris:
Numi, pietà del mio straziato core.
Egli è innocente, lo salvate, o Numi!
Disperato, tremendo è il mio dolore!

Amneris:
Gods, mercy on my tortured heart.
He is innocent, save him, oh gods!
My despairing sorrow is tremendous!

Radames, between Guards, passes and descends to the subterranean judgment hall.

Ramfis, Sacerdoti:
Spirito del Nume, sovra noi discendi!

Ramphis, Priests:
Spirit of the gods descend upon us!

Amneris:
Oh! chi lo salva! Mi sento morir! Ohimè!

Amneris:
Oh! Who will save him? Alas!

Ramfis:
Radamès! Radamès! Radamès!
Tu rivelasti della patria i segreti allo
straniero! Discolpati.

Ramphis:
Radames! Radames! Radames!
You revealed secrets of our country to the
foreigner! Defend yourself!

Sacerdoti:
Discolpati.

Priests:
Defend yourself.

Ramfis::
Egli tace.

Ramphis:
He is silent.

Ramfis, Sacerdoti::
Traditor!

Ramphis, Priests:
Traitor!

Amneris:
Ah, pietà! Egli è innocente! Numi, pietà!

Amneris:
Ah, mercy! He is innocent! Gods, mercy!

Ramfis:
Radames! Radames! Radames!
Tu disertasti dal campo il dì che precedea la
pugna.
Discolpati.

Ramphis:
Radames! Radames! Radames!
You deserted the camp the day preceding
the battle.
Defend yourself.

Sacerdoti:
Discolpati.

Priests:
Defend yourself.

Ramfis:
Egli tace.

Ramphis:
He is silent.

Ramfis, Sacerdoti:
Traditor!

Ramphis, Priests:
Traitor!

Amneris:
Ah, pietà! Ah! lo salvate! Numi, pietà!

Amneris:
Ah, mercy! Ah! Save him! Gods, mercy!

Ramfis:
Radames! Radames! Radames!
Tu fè violasti alla patria spergiuro, al Re,
all'onore.
Discolpati.

Ramphis:
Radames! Radames! Radames!
You violated the faith that you swore to
your country, to the King, and to honor.
Defend yourself.

Sacerdoti:
Discolpati.

Priests:
Defend yourself.

Ramfis:
Egli tace.

Ramphis:
He is silent.

Ramfis, Sacerdoti:
Traditor!

Ramphis, Priests:
Traitor!

Amneris:
Ah, pietà! Ah, lo salvate, Numi, pietà!

Amneris:
Ah, mercy! Ah, save him, Gods, mercy!

Ramfis, Sacerdoti:
Radames, è deciso il tuo fato.
Degli infami la morte tu avrai;
sotto l'ara del Nume sdegnato.
A te vivo fia schiuso l'avel.

Amneris:
A lui vivo la tomba! O, gl'infami!
N'e di sangue son paghi giammai.
E si chiaman ministri del ciel!

Ramfis, Sacerdoti:
Traditor! Traditor! Traditor!

Amneris:
Sacerdoti: compiste un delitto!
Tigri infami di sangue assetate.
Voi la terra ed i Numi oltraggiate.
Voi punite chi colpe non ha!

Ramfis:
È traditor!

Sacerdoti:
È traditor!

Ramfis, Sacerdoti:
Morrà!

Amneris:
Sacerdote: quest'uomo che uccidi
tu lo sai, da me un giorno fu amato.
L'anatema d'un core straziato
col suo sangue su te ricadrà!

Ramfis:
È traditor!

Sacerdoti:
È traditor!

Ramfis, Sacerdoti:
Morrà!

Ramphis, Priests:
Radames, your fate is decided.
You shall die like the infamous,
under the altar of the scorned gods.
You will be entombed alive.

Amneris:
Alive in a tomb! Oh, infamy!
They are never satisfied with blood,
and call themselves ministers of heaven!

Ramphis, Priests:
Traitor! Traitor! Traitor!

Amneris: (*Attacking the Priests who emerge from the subterranean hall*)
Priests: You have committed evil!
Infamous tigers thirsting for blood,
you outrage earth and the gods...
You punish an innocent!

Ramphis:
He is a traitor!

Priests:
He is a traitor!

Ramphis, Priests:
He shall die!

Amneris: (*to Ramphis*)
Priest: This man you kill,
you know one day was loved by me.
The curse of a broken heart.
His blood will fall upon you!

Ramphis!
He is a traitor!

Priests:
He is a traitor!

Ramphis, Priests:
He shall die!

Amneris:
Voi la terra ed i Numi oltraggiate,
Voi punite chi colpe non ha.
Ah no, non è traditor, pietà!

Amneris:
You outrage earth and the gods.
You punish an innocent!
Ah no, he is not a traitor, mercy!

Ramfis, Sacerdoti:
Morrà!
È traditor! Morrà!
Traditor! Traditor! Traditor!

Ramphis, Priests:
He will die!
He is a traitor! He will die!
Traitor! Traitor! Traitor!

Amneris:
Empia razza! Anatema su voi!
La vendetta del ciel scenderà!
Anatema su voi!

Amneris:
Impious race! A curse on you!
Let heaven's vengeance fall on you!
A curse on you!

ACT IV - Scene 2

The scene is divided into two floors, the upper the Interior of the Temple of Vulcan, the lower a subterranean crypt.

Radames::
La fatal pietra sovra me si chiuse...
Ecco la tomba mia. Del dì la luce più non
vedrò... Non revedrò più Aida.

Aida, ove sei tu?
Possa tu almeno viver felice e la mia sorte
orrenda sempre ignorar!
Qual gemito! Una larva! Una vision! No!
Forma umana è questa.
Ciel! Aida!

Radames:
The fatal stone above me is closed..
This is my tomb. I shall no more see the
light of day. I shall see no more. I shall not
see Aida again.
Aida, Where are you?
May you at least live happily and never
know of my dreadful fate.
A groan! A ghost! A vision..
No! It is a human form.
Heavens! Aida!

Aida:
Son io.

Aida:
It is I.

Radames:
Tu... in questa tomba!

Radames:
You...in this tomb!

Aida:
Presago il core della tua condanna,
in questa tomba che per te s'apriva
Io penetrai furtiva. E qui lontana da ogni
umano sguardo nelle tue braccia desiai
morire.

Aida:
My heart knew of your sentence to be
condemned into this tomb.I made my way
here far from all. I yearn to die in your
arms.

Radames:
Morir! Sì pura e bella!
Morir per me d'amore...
Degli anni tuoi nel fiore fuggir la vita!
T'avea il cielo per l'amor creata,
ed io t'uccido per averti amata!
No, non morrai!
Troppo t'amai!
Troppo sei bella!

Radames:
To die! So pure and beautiful!
To die for love for me...
in the flower of your youth!
Heaven created you for love,
and I kill you for having loved me!
No, you shall not die!
I loved you too much!
You are too beautiful!

Aida:
Vedi? Di morte l'angelo
radiante a noi s'appressa.
Ne adduce eterni gaudi sovra i suoi vanni
d'or.
Già veggo il ciel dischiudersi,
ivi ogni affanno cessa.
Ivi comincia l'estasi d'un immortale amor.

Aida:
Look! The radiant angel of death approaches us.
He takes us under his golden feathers to
eternal joys.
Already the heavens open,
and there every grief ceases.
There the ecstasy of an immortal love begins.

Sacerdotesse:
Immenso Fthà, del mondo.
Spirito animator...

Priestesses: *(in the temple above)*
All-powerful Phthà, spiritual animator of
the world.......

Sacerdoti:
Ah!

Priests:
Ah!

Aida:
Triste canto!

Aida:
A sad song!

Radames:
Il tripudio dei Sacerdoti.

Radames:
The jubilation of the Priests.

Aida:
Il nostro inno di morte.

Aida:
Our hymn of death.

Radames:
Né le mie forti braccia smuoverti potranno,
o fatal pietra!

Radames: *(trying to move the stone)*
My strong arms cannot move the stone, o
fatal stone!

Sacerdoti, Sacerdotesse:
Ah! Noi t'invochiamo, t'invochiam.

Priests, Priestesses:
Ah! We invoke you!, we invoke you.

Aida:
Invan! Tutto è finito sulla terra per noi.

Aida:
It is in vain. All is over for us on earth.

Radames:
È vero! È vero!

Radames:
It is true! It is true!

Meno mosso

O terra ad - di - o, addi - o val - le di pian - ti,

Aida e Radames:
O terra addio addio valle di pianti.
Sogno di gaudio che in dolor svanì.
A noi si schiude il ciel e l'alme erranti
Volano al raggio dell'interno dì.

Aida and Radames:
Farewell earth, farewell valleys of tears.
Dreams of joy that vanish in grief.
Heavens open to us, wandering souls who
fly to the rays of eternal day.

Sacerdoti, Sacerdotesse:
Immenso Fthà, noi t'invochiam!

Priests, Priestesses:
All-powerful Phthà, we invoke you!

Aida e Radames:
Ah! Si schiude il ciel.
O terra addio; addio valli di pianti...

Aida and Radames:
Ah The heavens open.
Farewell earth, farewell valleys of tears.

Amneris:

Amneris:
*(in the temple above, prostrate on the
stone that closes the vault)*
Pace t'imploro...
I pray for peace for you...

Aida e Radames:
Sogno di gaudio che in dolor svanì.

Aida and Radames:
Dreams of joy that vanish in grief.

Amneris:
... salma adorata.

Amneris:
........adored corpse.

Aida e Radames:
A noi si schiude il ciel...

Aida and Radames:
The heavens open for us.

Amneris:
Isi placata...

Amneris:
Isis is appeased.

Aida e Radames:
Si schiude il ciel e l'alme erranti...

Aida and Radames:
The heavens open for wandering souls.

Amneris:
Isi placata ti schiuda il ciel!

Amneris:
Isis is appeased and the heavens open!

Aida e Radames:
Volano al raggio dell'eterno dì.

Aida and Radames:
Wandering souls who fly to the rays of eternal day.

Sacerdoti e Sacerdotesse:
Noi t'invochiam...

Priests and Priestesses:
We invoke you...

Aida e Radames:
Il ciel...

Aida and Radames:
Heaven.

Sacerdoti e Sacerdotesse:
Immenso Fthà!

Priests and Priestesses:
All-powerful Phthà!

Aida e Radames:
Si schiude il ciel!

Aida and Radames:
Heaven opens!

(Aida falls and dies in Radames's arms)

Amneris:
Pace t'imploro, ... pace, pace...... pace!

Amneris:
I pray for peace, ...peace, peace, peace!

Sacerdoti, Sacerdotesse:
Immenso Fthà!

Priests, Priestesses:
All-powerful Phthà!

FINE

THE END